Tell Me about When Moms and Dads Go to Jail

Judi Goozh and Sue Jeweler

Jessica Kingsley Publishers
London and Philadelphia

All images reproduced under the terms of the Creative Commons Attribution 2.0 Generic license with thanks to the photographers.
Page 10: Cliff, Wikimedia Commons
Page 14 and 15: PlayLab, Inc.
Page 24: Kathrin Rieger, Flickr
Page 27: Carissa Rogers, Flickr

First published in 2018
by Jessica Kingsley Publishers
73 Collier Street
London N1 9BE, UK
and
400 Market Street, Suite 400
Philadelphia, PA 19106, USA

www.jkp.com

Library of Congress Cataloging in Publication Data
A CIP catalog record for this book is available from the Library of Congress

British Library Cataloguing in Publication Data
A CIP catalogue record for this book is available from the British Library

ISBN 978 1 78592 807 9
eISBN 978 1 78450 842 5

Printed and bound in China

Tell Me about When Moms and Dads Go to Jail

also in the Tell Me about Jail series

Tell Me about When Moms and Dads Come Home from Jail
Judi Goozh and Sue Jeweler
ISBN 978 1 78592 806 2
eISBN 978 1 78450 843 2

of related interest

The Boy Who Built a Wall Around Himself
Ali Redford
Illustrated by Kara Simpson
ISBN 978 1 84905 683 0
eISBN 978 1 78450 200 3

Can I tell you about Loneliness?
A guide for friends, family and professionals
Julian Stern
Illustrated by Helen Lees
ISBN 978 1 78592 243 5
eISBN 978 1 78450 526 4

How Sprinkle the Pig Escaped the River of Tears
A Story About Being Apart From Loved Ones
Anne Westcott and C. C. Alicia Hu
Introduced by Pat Ogden
ISBN 978 1 78592 769 0
eISBN 978 1 78450 669 8
Hidden Strengths Therapeutic Children's Books series

The Healthy Coping Colouring Book and Journal
Creative Activities to Help Manage Stress, Anxiety and Other Big Feelings
Pooky Knightsmith
Illustrated by Emily Hamilton
ISBN 978 1 78592 139 1
eISBN 978 1 78450 405 2

Trauma is Really Strange
Steve Haines
Art by Sophie Standing
ISBN 978 1 84819 293 5
eISBN 978 0 85701 240 1
...is Really Strange series

We dedicate this book to the children with an incarcerated parent and their families, who struggle each and every day, and to the professionals who are dedicated to helping them through difficult times.

We also dedicate this book to our families—our husbands, Paul and Larry, and our children and grandchildren.

Acknowledgments

Our journey on behalf of children with an incarcerated parent has been guided and supported by many. In 2007, our mentor, Art Wallenstein, who was the Director of Maryland's Montgomery County Department of Correction and Rehabilitation, made it possible to create a project to raise awareness about this often-overlooked and underserved population. Robert Green, as warden of Maryland's Montgomery County Clarksburg Facility (MCCF), offered great support as well. Kendra Jochum, LCSW-C Reentry Services Manager at MCCF, worked tirelessly and made incredible contributions to this effort. Randall Wylie provided the important photographs from MCCF that show the reality of jail so that children can see the real-life, real-world situation for a parent. From the beginning, Dr. Craig Uchida saw the importance of this issue and offered us tremendous support and continues his own work for children with an incarcerated parent. Jeff Franklin and Archie Coates, creators of PlayLab, Inc., have been with us every step of the way to give our writing an appropriate visual format. Cindy Perlis, Director of *Art for Recovery* for the UCSF Comprehensive Cancer Center at Mount Zion, gave us her creative insight and guidance on these books.

James Cherry, Editor at Jessica Kingsley Publishers, Ltd., gave us a fabulous home for our work. His enthusiastic support for this book has been an inspiration. His warmth and professionalism have been stellar and we thank him for the opportunity to highlight issues for children with an incarcerated parent. Editorial Assistant Daisy Watt has shown patience and support throughout the entire process of publication.

To the Reader

This book will help you understand what is happening to your mom or dad who goes to jail.

Tell Me about When Moms and Dads Go to Jail tells a story about a child like you who finds out that Dad has been arrested and is in jail. You may have many questions about what will happen and, throughout the story, these questions are answered.

Moms are arrested and go to jail, too. Even though the story is about a child and a dad, the same story, questions, and answers are true if your mom goes to jail.

You may have a lot of different feelings about the situation, from sadness, worry and confusion to anger and not wanting to be with anyone. All your emotions are normal. Feelings are not right or wrong—they just are!

Tell Me about When Moms and Dads Go to Jail

We were out walking. A police car stopped and looked at my dad. Soon there were lots of police cars and flashing lights. I was scared. I wondered what was happening.

The police officers talked to my dad. They put handcuffs on him like in the movies and put him in the back seat of a police car. Another police officer talked to Mom. A police officer asked me questions. I felt confused.

Where is Dad going? I wondered if they would take Mom, too. Who would take care of me? Will I have to live with Grandma? When will Dad come back?

We went home. Dad didn't come back. I didn't say goodbye or hug or kiss him. I felt sad and worried. I love Dad. I don't know where he went. He just disappeared.

Where was Dad? I was afraid. Mom said that Dad did something really bad and he had to go in the police car to jail. She said he might not come back for a while.

I couldn't sleep. I had very bad dreams all night. There were questions floating in my head.

Why do people go to jail? Mom said that in school and at home, you have rules to follow. Listen to your teachers. Don't hurt anyone. Don't take things that belong to someone else.

Grown-ups have rules, too. They are called laws. You cannot drive until you pass a test to have a driver's license. You cannot hurt children. You cannot steal. You cannot fight.

DO NOT

HURT CHILDREN

STEAL

FIGHT

DRIVE WITHOUT A LICENSE

Mom also told me that when you make a mistake in school or at home and do not follow the rules, there are consequences or punishments. For example, you might get a time out. You might need to tell the other person you are sorry. You cannot watch TV or play with your toys.

When grown-ups don't follow the rules and laws, there are big consequences or punishments. When grown-ups don't do what a law says, they might have to go to jail.

Laws keep us all safe. We need to follow the rules and laws.

Dad is in jail. He broke the law and has to face the consequences. I feel so sad.

Mom told me lots of things about jail.

What does jail look like? The jail is a big building with lots of rooms and gates that open and close. There is a big wire fence around the building. The people who are sent to jail live there until they are released.

Where does he sleep? Everyone lives in a cell. It is a small room with a bed, a shelf, a sink, a toilet, and a desk. He sleeps on a bunk bed, with a bed on the bottom and a bed on top. He might even have to share the room with someone else.

Where does he eat? He walks to a room in the jail called a day room. He goes through a kitchen line where the food workers give him something to eat on a tray. It is kind of like the cafeteria at school. Then he goes and sits at a table.

What does he do all day? Jail is not fun. Dad has to follow the rules and cannot leave the building. He can go to a computer lab or learn in a classroom. He can work at a job in the jail. He can go to a vocational class and learn skills for a new job. He can talk to someone to learn how to deal with his problems. He can talk to someone to learn how to be a better parent. He gets to go outside in the fresh air in a cover-enclosed recreation yard.

Is he safe? The people in uniforms at the jail are called correctional officers. Their job is to keep him safe.

There are other people who work at the jail like counselors, teachers, doctors, and nurses. They take care of Dad.

What does he wear? Dad doesn't get to wear his own clothes from home. Everyone has to wear a uniform called a jumpsuit.

What happens if he is hurt or sick? He can visit the doctors or nurses in the jail. They will give him medicine if he needs it.

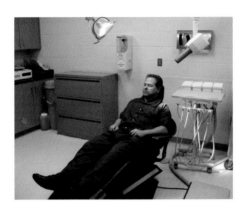

I am worried. **Do I go to school tomorrow? Is this a secret? What do I tell my friends?**

Mom said that when a mom or dad goes to jail everyone in the family is upset. Some things in families are private. People in the family can talk about them, but usually people do not tell everyone else. People in families need to talk to each other to decide together who to tell about Mom or Dad being in jail.

Mom says we can visit Dad in jail. I miss him. I want to see him, but I am scared again. **Will I see him as soon as I get to jail? Can I bring him something? Can we have lunch together? Can I hug him?**

Mom told me that every jail is a little different. First, you tell a correctional officer your name and who you are visiting. You put everything you are carrying in a locker. You cannot bring anything to your mom or dad—no books, no magazines, no pictures, and no food. Then you walk through a metal detector, which is like an entrance gate that can check to see if a person is carrying in a knife or a gun.

You wait in a big visiting room until someone says you can visit. When you see your dad, he is behind a glass window. You pick up a phone to talk to him. You cannot hug, kiss, or touch him.

Visiting was hard. I want him to get out so we can be together. **When will he leave?** Mom is not sure. I am mad. It is not fair!

What can I do? Mom says I can do a lot of things. I can talk to her and someone like the counselor at school. I can keep a journal, write letters, and send my picture and cards to Dad. I can talk to him on the phone if he calls me, but I cannot call him. Not all parents write or call, but I know Dad still loves me even if he doesn't call.

I sometimes feel angry that Dad left me. I am angry at the police for putting Dad in jail. Mom said that they were doing their job. It is not their fault that Dad is in jail.

I wonder if it is my fault. Mom says it is not my fault. I wonder what will happen. I feel nervous. I worry about Dad. Mom says that Dad worries about me, too.

Even though I am afraid, sad, and angry, I still hope that when Dad gets out we can see each other. Mom told me that Dad is working hard to change. There are special programs that will help him when he gets out. I hope he won't get in trouble and go back to jail. Whatever happens, I will be okay.

Activities for Children

Expressing thoughts and feelings through writing and drawing is helpful. Writing poems or stories or a collection of sentences and drawing pictures can be ways to share your feelings. Writing and drawing can make you feel less stressed and even put you in a better mood.

It might not be easy for you to say what you think and feel in a conversation. Writing and drawing are other ways you can share what is in your mind and heart.

Writing Activity

DIRECTIONS

If you wish, you can write about your ideas and feelings on a piece of paper or even keep a journal. You may write a poem or a story or the lyrics to a song or just some sentences. There are no grades when you write and it will feel really good when you can let people know how you feel or let them read the words you write.

Some Ideas You Might Want to Write About

- How did you feel when the police came?

- Where did you think your mom or dad was going?

- How is your life different now?

- I want my mom or dad to know _____.

- What do you want to say to your friends when they ask about your mom or dad?

- What do you want to say to your teacher, counselor, clergy, or someone else important to you when they ask about your mom or dad?

- Make a list of what is bothering you and how you can feel better.

- Make a list of all the people in your life that can help you feel safe.

- Make a list of all the good things in your life.

- Make a list of all the things you would like to say to your mom or dad.

Drawing Activity

DIRECTIONS

If you wish, you can draw a picture about your ideas and feelings on a piece of paper. It is okay to only use color or lines to express your feelings. You may use symbols (like a sun or a heart) or stick figures. You can pick a color that describes your feelings and just color in the whole page. There are no grades when you draw and it will feel really good when you can show people how you feel.

Some Ideas You Might Want to Draw a Picture About

- This is how I feel.

- Draw a picture of how you imagine your mom or dad in jail.

- Draw a picture of your feelings (angry, sad, lonely, or another feeling) for your mom or dad.

- Draw a picture of all the good things in your life.

- Draw a picture of your family and send it to your mom or dad in jail.

Tips for Parents and Professionals

Introduction

According to a Department of Justice report from the year 2007, 2.3 percent of children in the United States (nearly 1.7 million children) had an incarcerated parent. On any given day more than 7 million children may have a parent in prison or jail or under parole or probation supervision. Twenty-two percent of these children are under five years old. About two-thirds of teens whose mothers have arrest histories also have fathers with arrest histories. It is reported that the number of children who have a mother in prison has more then doubled since 1991.

These children, who are victims of their parent's crimes, are often afraid and confused by the changes in their own lives. Their families may have to move. There may be a loss of income. There may be exposure to negative influences prior to the arrest, such as domestic violence or drugs. They may feel stigma and shame from friends, neighbors, and even relatives. Unfortunately, this often leads to a cycle of further issues, including difficulty in the social, emotional, and behavioral areas of life and school.

If you are reading this book, you may have someone in your family who is incarcerated and want to learn more about what happens to that family member in jail and what you can say or do to help yourself and others.

With support and intervention from professionals, the child and family can learn how to cope. Each family's circumstances are unique. We hope that this book helps you to understand more about the issue, become more sensitive to the needs of the child, and use some of the activities to create a more positive experience.

If you are a professional or caregiver working with a child who has an incarcerated parent, we hope that this book gives you an opportunity to answer questions a child may have, as well as to open the door for conversation.

WHY USE THIS BOOK?
Kids Who Have a Parent in Jail

- This book will give you honest answers about what happens when your parent is arrested and goes to jail.

- This book may give you information so that you can talk to someone who can help you.

- This book will give you a chance to write about your feelings or draw a picture that shows how you feel.

Anyone with an Incarcerated Relative

- This book will help you explain what is happening to the child's parent.

- This book will help you initiate a meaningful discussion with the child.

Professionals Who Serve this Population

- This book is a resource to use in conjunction with counseling, therapy, and any other service you offer to a child experiencing parental incarceration.

- This book will help you explain what is happening to the child's parent.

- This book will help you initiate a meaningful discussion with the child.

HOW TO USE THIS BOOK

- Read the book.

- Look at the photographs.

- Think about the questions and the answers.

- Talk to a person about your thoughts and feelings.

- Write or draw about your thoughts and feelings.

- Ask any other questions you may have.

GUIDING DISCUSSION QUESTIONS FOR KIDS, FAMILIES, CAREGIVERS, AND PROFESSIONALS WHO SERVE THIS POPULATION

- What are you thinking and feeling because Mom or Dad is not home?

- What are you worried or scared about?

- What would you say to a friend at school if they wanted to know the whereabouts of your mom or dad?

- Would you like some help to talk about what you could say to your friends?

- Do you have any other questions?

Helpful Hints for School-Aged Children with an Incarcerated Parent

These are ideas that children and families may use as they navigate through the issues related to parental incarceration.

Children who have an incarcerated parent feel the same level of trauma as children who have had a parent die or whose parents have divorced. The children may exhibit aggression, defiance, disobedience, depression, anxiety, and/or withdrawal. Younger children may show withdrawal and anger, especially to the person taking care of them.

If there are many other losses, such as losing the income of the other parent, changing homes, losing friends, having to move, or having to live with a grandparent or another relative, then the child may experience even more behavior issues. Even if the child stays with the other parent, he or she may have to cope with social stigma, stress in the family, and, often, feelings of shame.

Sometimes the parent or caregiver is so overwhelmed with all of the issues they have to deal with that the children's needs are ignored.

School-aged children may have additional problems with school work and issues with their peers. They may be very reluctant to discuss their feelings and often maintain a facade that everything is okay. These same children may experience low self-esteem.

Research shows that school professionals can be critical in making sure that children who have an incarcerated parent are properly assessed and supported.

The following strategies may be helpful to the adult who spends time with a child who is impacted by the incarceration of a parent. Use this list personally or share it with someone who could benefit from the ideas.

- Ask open-ended questions that will not just be answered by yes or no. Some examples are:

  › How do you feel because Mom or Dad is not home?

  › What are the things that worry you?

  › What would you say if someone at school or your friend asked you about your mom or dad?

- When your child talks to you:

  › Try to be a good listener.

  › Parrot back what your child says. For example:

  Child: I feel scared at night.

  Parent or caregiver: I wonder what you are scared about.

  › Be aware of your body language:

  Make eye contact.

  Be aware of your facial expressions.

  › Keep an open mind.

- When you talk to your child:

  › Be honest.

  › Be calm. Model self-control.

  › Be patient.

  › Be consistent about rules.

> › Encourage your child to express anger by using words.

> › Use "I Messages." For example:

>> This is not an "I Message": You never clean up after yourself.

>> This is an "I Message": I get upset and frustrated when I pick up your toys after you play with them.

- Tell the school staff personnel with whom you feel comfortable about what is happening to you and your family. Share the impact of your situation, especially if the child is acting out or displaying depression. (Talk to the counselor, teacher, principal, speech and language pathologist, special education teacher or case manager, or any staff member with whom you are comfortable.)

- Talk to your family doctor or someone at your clinic or urgent care facility.

- Contact agencies or organizations for help.

- Find positive and healthy outlets for you and your child, such as helping others or keeping a journal.

- Foster a positive relationship between your child and the incarcerated parent.

For further information or comments and suggestions, feel free to contact us through our website: www.creativefamilyprojects.org

Handling Conflict

Conflicts happen in our lives. Triggers are the verbal and non-verbal actions that can start a confrontation with another person or group. In order to understand our triggers, we need to understand the warning signs and how we can recognize them in ourselves and others. We also need to understand coping mechanisms. They are the actions we can take to increase the amount of think time and cooling-off time between recognizing we've been triggered and taking an inappropriate action. Using coping mechanisms can change a negative response to one that is positive. In this way, conflicts can be avoided.

CONFLICT-RESOLUTION
Triggers

Verbal Triggers
Get out of my face!
It's your fault!

Warning Signs
Hands sweating
Heart pounding

Non-Verbal Triggers
Rolling your eyes
Holding up a fist

Mind racing
Red-faced

Reactions
Negative reaction

Coping mechanisms
Take deep breaths
Count to ten
Take a walk

Reactions
Positive reaction

ATFRC: ACTION/THOUGHTS/FEELINGS/ REACTION/CONSEQUENCE

Each of us is in control of our behavior. We make choices about our behavior based on our thoughts, feelings, and motivations at the time. Changing our thoughts can lead to different feelings, reactions, and consequences. Developing this "habit of mind" can help create more productive resolutions to conflicts.

ACTION	**ACTION**
THOUGHTS	**CHANGE THOUGHTS**
FEELINGS	**FEELINGS CHANGE**
REACTION	**REACTION CHANGES**
CONSEQUENCE	**DIFFERENT CONSEQUENCE**

Example for understanding how ATFRC works:

ACTION	**ACTION**
The child picks up a book.	The child picks up a book.
THOUGHTS	**CHANGE THOUGHTS**
The child thinks, "It's my fault my dad went to jail."	The child thinks, "It's my fault my dad went to jail. Mom told me it is not my fault. Dad broke the law."
FEELINGS	**FEELINGS CHANGE**
The child feels angry.	The child feels sad.
REACTION	**REACTION CHANGES**
The child throws a book across the room and breaks a lamp.	The child puts the book back on the table.
CONSEQUENCE	**DIFFERENT CONSEQUENCE**
The mom punishes the child.	The mom sees that the child is sad and gives him a hug.

IMPACT OF JAIL VISITS ON CHILDREN

Without visits, children may believe their incarcerated parent no longer loves them or cares about them.

Some research says that visiting increases the likelihood that the relationship will survive when the parent is released. Some families, however, feel visiting a parent in jail is too traumatic.

Things to Consider During the Visit

- Your child may feel nervous or scared or worried.

- Because your child may have changed since the last visit, he or she may have different concerns and feelings.

- Your child may be uncomfortable talking to the parent in jail and may need other ways to comfortably communicate, like writing or drawing a picture.

- Deciding on the best time to visit may impact how your child feels during the visit.

- Saying goodbye after the visit may be difficult for your child. Try to give your child a few minutes before the end of the visit so that he or she can start mentally preparing to leave.

Things to Consider After the Visit

- When your child leaves, he or she may be sad, tired, and tearful or engage in aggressive behavior.

- It is very important for your child to be able to express his or her feelings about the visit. Families and other individuals can be a great support system. Consider talking to the social worker for advice and assistance.

- There may be programs or resources that can help you and your child through this time. Ask the social worker if there are any mentoring programs or other resources that can be of assistance.

WHERE TO GO FOR HELP

- School counselors and teachers

- Social workers

- Pediatricians

- Community agencies, including Health and Human Services, Mental Health Association, Child Welfare

- Churches and other religious houses of worship

- Professional colleagues

- Additional, appropriate resources at the library or online

Resources and Further Reading

WEBSITES

The Annie E. Casey Foundation

Children of Incarcerated Parents Fact Sheet
www.aecf.org/resources/children-of-incarcerated-parents-fact-sheet
This fact sheet presents data on parents as prisoners, the affect this has on the children and how foster care plays a role.

Ensuring Success for Children with Incarcerated Parents
www.aecf.org/resources/ensuring-success-for-children-with-incarcerated-parents
This discussion guide shares statistics, solutions, and next steps for funders interested in aiding children of incarcerated parents.

Creative Family Projects, LLC

www.creativefamilyprojects.org
Creative Family Projects, LLC identifies problems and provides solutions by synthesizing information from organizations, institutions, and corporations into booklets and training modules for the benefit of children, youth, and families.

"Echoes of Incarceration"

www.echoesofincarceration.org
This film, produced by teens with incarcerated parents, intercuts the stories of four young people with the voices of experts and advocates in the field, and creates an emotional, compelling case for the importance of ongoing parental contact.

For Children in Foster Care
Partnerships Between Corrections and Child Welfare
www.aecf.org/resources/partnerships-between-corrections-and-child-welfare-collaboration-for-change
Partnerships Between Corrections and Child Welfare: Collaboration for Change, Part Two explores the gap between the systems, which results in tremendous hardship on children, caretakers, families and workers in both places, and what can be done to improve coordination without a great deal of additional funding.

Foreverfamily
http://foreverfam.org
Foreverfamily works to ensure that, no matter what the circumstances, all children have the opportunity to be surrounded by the love of family. The organization focuses on providing services to children with incarcerated parents and their families.

The National Resource Center on Children and Families of the Incarcerated
Download helpful materials for service providers and families.

Children of Incarcerated Parents Library
http://nrccfi.camden.rutgers.edu/resources/library/children-of-prisoners-library

Age-Specific Guidance
Caring for Children of Incarcerated Parents
http://nrccfi.camden.rutgers.edu/files/cipl201-caringforcip.pdf

Advice for Caregivers
Questions from Caregivers
http://nrccfi.camden.rutgers.edu/files/cipl202-questionsfromcaregivers.pdf

Tips from Caregivers for Caregivers
http://nrccfi.camden.rutgers.edu/files/cpl204-tipsfromcaregivers.pdf

The New Jersey Department of Corrections
"What about me?" When a parent goes to prison: A guide to discussing your incarceration with your children
www.state.nj.us/corrections/pdf/OTS/InmateFamilyResources/WhatAboutMe.pdf
Preparing children for prison visits.

The Oregon Program
"Parenting Inside Out"
www.parentinginsideout.org
www.parentinginsideout.org/resources
An evidence-based curriculum for incarcerated mothers and fathers, including a set of materials targeted toward educators and caregivers and a collection of resources for children.

Sesame Street
Little Children, Big Challenges: Incarceration
www.sesamestreet.org/toolkits/incarceration
A series of online toolkits for children and their parents dealing with adversity. Issues include not just prison, but also bullying, divorce, and relocation. The toolkit contains videos, activities, and handouts offering advice, encouragement, and games for when they visit Mom or Dad in jail.

Youth.gov
Children of Incarcerated Parents
http://youth.gov/youth-topics/children-of-incarcerated-parents
For more information and resources on these overlapping problems, please see the additional links and resources at this site.

PUBLICATIONS

We suggest exploring the Internet and public libraries for books about children with an incarcerated parent.

Barnes-Robinson, L. and Jeweler, S. (2007). Conflict resolution: Teaching Conflict Resolution and Mediation through the Curriculum. Hawthorne, NJ: Educational Impressions, Inc.

Bouchet, S.M. (2008). Children and Families with Incarcerated Parents. Annie E. Casey Foundation.

Christian, S. (2009). Children of Incarcerated Parents. National Conference of State Legislatures.

Correia, M.E. "Determinants of attitudes toward police of Latino immigrants and non-immigrants." Retrieved October 13, 2010. http://www.sciencedirect.com/science?_ob=ArticleURL&udi=B6V

Gable, S. (1992). "Children of incarcerated and criminal parents: Adjustment, behavior, and prognosis." Bull Am Acad Psychiatry Law, 20 (1), 89-113.

Glaze, L.E. and Maruschak, L.M. (2008). Parents in Prison and Their Children. U.S. Department of Justice, Bureau of Justice Statistics. Washington, DC: Government Printing Office.

Hairston, C.F. (2007). Focus on Children with Incarcerated Parents. Annie E. Casey Foundation.

Jucovy, L. (2003). Amachi: Mentoring Children of Prisoners in Philadelphia. Philadelphia, PA: Public/Private Ventures.

La Vigne, N.G. (2008). Broken Bonds: Understanding and Addressing the Needs of Children with Incarcerated Parents. Annie E. Casey Foundation.

Montgomery County Public Schools (1994). Conflict Resolution Tools: Elementary Version, Teaching Through the Curriculum. Rockville, MD: Author.

Mumola, C.J. (2000). Bureau of Justice Statistics Special Report: Incarcerated Parents and Their Children. Washington, DC: U.S. Department of Justice [NCJ 182335].

Mumola, C.J. (2002). "1996 Survey of Inmates in Local Jails, 1997 Survey of Inmates in State and Federal Correctional Facilities, 2001 Annual Survey of Jails, and 2001 National Prisoners Statistics Program." (Presented at the National Center for Children and Families, Washington, DC, October 31, 2002.)

Nickel, J., Garland, C. and Kane, L. (2009). Children of Incarcerated Parents: An Action Plan for Federal Policymakers. New York: Council of State Governments Justice Center.

Parke, R. and Clarke-Stewart, K. A. (2002). "Effects of parental incarceration on young children." (Paper prepared for the "From Prison to Home" conference.)

Petras, D. D., Derozotes, D. M. and Wills, S. (1999). Parent-Child Bonding and Attachment: Research Implications for Child Welfare Practice. Dialogues on Child Welfare Issues. Chicago, IL: University of Illinois at Chicago, Jane Addams Center for Social Policy and Research.

Ramiro, M. (2007). "Incorporating Latinos and immigrants into policing research." Criminology & Public Policy, 6 (1), 57–64.

Resources and interventions for children of incarcerated parents. (2008). Baltimore, MD. University of Maryland School of Social Work.

Zimmer, J.A. (1998). Let's Say: "We can work it out!" Problem Solving Through Mediation Ages 8-13. Culver City, CA: Social Studies School Service.